# An Old Fashioned Budget

## Books by Mrs. White

For the Love of Christian Homemaking: *Pleasant Visits from My Parlour*

Mother's Book of Home Economics: *Remembrances, Letters, and Essays from a New England Housewife*

Living on His Income: *Remembrances and Advice for the Christian Housewife*

Economy for the Christian Home: *A 12 - Week Challenge for Wives to Increase Charitable Giving*

Mother's Hour: *Encouragement from Home for the Christian Housewife*

At Mother's House: *The Blessing of Being a Christian Housewife*

Introduction to Home Economics: *Gentle Instruction to Find Joy in Christian Homemaking*

Early Morning Revival Challenge: *90 - day Bible Study program*

Old Fashioned Motherhood: *Baby and Child Care Advice from a New England Housewife*

{Cover photograph taken in Manchester, Vermont, 2019, by Mrs. White – A writing desk in the sitting room of Mrs. Robert Lincoln's historic summer mansion.}

**An Old Fashioned Budget**

# An Old Fashioned Budget

Humble Financial Management for the Christian Housewife

By Mrs. Sharon White

The Legacy of Home Press
**puritanlight@gmail.com**

*An Old Fashioned Budget*
Copyright 2019 by Mrs. Sharon White

All Rights Reserved.

No portion of this book may be copied without permission from the publisher.

The Legacy of Home Press

ISBN - 978-0-578-61018-4

*An Old Fashioned Budget: Humble Financial Management for the Christian Housewife*

Author – Mrs. Sharon White

**An Old Fashioned Budget**

# Contents

Chapter 1
    Introduction . . . . . . . . . . . . . . . . . . . . . .     7

Chapter 2
    The Chosen . . . . . . . . . . . . . . . . . . . . . .     10

Chapter 3
    A Simple Budget . . . . . . . . . . . . . . . . .     12

Chapter 4
    We'll Get By . . . . . . . . . . . . . . . . . . . . . .     17

Chapter 5
    Yankee Thrift . . . . . . . . . . . . . . . . . . . . .     24

Chapter 6
    Bookkeeping for the Home . . . . . . . . . .     31

Chapter 7
    Money Diary . . . . . . . . . . . . . . . . . . . . . .     37

Chapter 8
    The Writing Desk . . . . . . . . . . . . . . . . . .     46

Chapter 9
## The Old Fashioned Budget. . . . . . . . . . . .  54

Chapter 10
## A Trusted and Diligent Bookkeeper. . . . .  62

## Appendix  . . . . . . . . . . . . . . . . . . . .  69

### Photograph one
*Journal and Budget Book*. . . . . . . . . . .  71

### Photograph two
*Two Part Budget* . . . . . . . . . . . . . . . .  73

### Photograph three
*Spending Journal*. . . . . . . . . . . . . . . .  75

# Introduction

## 1

There is a great deal of information available about managing money and creating a budget. These are often geared towards higher income families who are rising financially and are moving up in success. While these are good things to do, I don't see very much help for the more common, old fashioned families, who are living on limited means. There are many households with a mother who stays home and lives on her husband's income. This seems rare these days, but was a traditional way of life just a few generations ago.

These small income households are not building wealth, seeking investments, or finding ways to increase income. Realistically speaking, there are many who are not likely to move up to a "higher" (in the world's standard) class of living. They strive to be productive, earn enough to provide for the family, and be grateful to the Lord for all they have been provided with.

There are many people who live in "American poverty" by government standards. But they have enough and manage well living simply. There are others who are in dire straits who are just trying to dig their way out of debt because of catastrophe, crisis, disability, or some disaster that could not be avoided. Whatever the reason for living on a small income, it is necessary to find a way to manage that money.

There is a method I present in this book that I will call, "bookkeeping for the home." It is the behind-the-scenes work that keeps the household functioning. It is the quiet, modest work that is necessary in every business but often neglected in the home.

In order to be content despite humble surroundings one has to learn to find joy in living on less. It is important to find happiness in our way of life without the use of much money. These will be the things we do with our time. It is old fashioned living that can help us live peacefully and gratefully with humble finances. In my childhood home, I never heard my parents talk about building wealth, getting rich, finding investments, or taking on extra work like we hear so much about these days. We just simply enjoyed our daily routine of school, work, the dinner hour, working in the yard, going to the park, or walking to the ocean (in my Massachusetts neighborhood).

There was a modest income provided by my father's "blue collar" laboring job. He was home each day before 4 in the afternoon. He was home each evening and all weekend long. My mother stayed home with us, like most mothers in those days. We children had chores and responsibilities we were required to do. The focus was

**An Old Fashioned Budget**

on the beauty and routine of home life. This precious way of living is possible on a small income if we take the time to manage the money well and avoid the modern hobby of spending it all while saving nothing.

One important thing to realize is that it is easier to earn money than it is to save it. I believe it was Benjamin Franklin who said, in his "Poor Richard Almanack" (1700's), something like, "A penny saved is a penny earned." We really need to remember what it was like generations ago when saving money was a common way of life. I have also heard of some wealthy families, who have passed their money down through the generations, and have taught their decedents that money is a responsibility and should not be spent. (I believe they meant to avoid waste and frivolity.) Whether one is rich or poor, it is old-time thinking to be careful with our money.

In this book I will share ideas for frugal living. I will explain how to start a financial journal (or money diary) as a bookkeeping tool to carefully monitor the household spending. I will describe, in detail, how to set up an old fashioned, modest budget without using modern categories of spending that were unheard of by humble families in previous generations. I will share some examples using fictitious families with either the wife or husband managing the money. If we can practice the art of old fashioned bookkeeping for the home, we will find such peace and contentment in everyday, humble living.

# The Chosen

## 2

It used to be very common for a husband to handle all financial matters. He may have been a business man who was used to running an office. He wanted to provide for his bride and keep her happy. He did not want her to worry about trials, or difficulties, that would happen throughout the years. He wanted to solve those problems, find solutions, and take pride in caring for his home and family with judicious skill. He wanted to make it in the world by managing his home and money in an honorable way.

The person who manages the money in business, or in a home, should be trustworthy. This person is taking on an important honor. This money manager ought to be known as one with integrity, one who could be trusted, and one who could be counted on through good times and bad.

At the same time, there is a level of skill and knowledge which is required to carefully handle bills, income, and expenses. Some have taken business courses to learn how to keep the books. Others have learned through experience and the study of books. In any case, it is important to learn how to manage money.

**An Old Fashioned Budget**

In many homes, these days, the wife is chosen to handle the finances. I like to think of this as a privilege. I compare it to the serving of tea. It has been said that First Lady Eleanor Roosevelt hosted many teas in the White House, while her husband was president of the United States. The Chief Usher remarked that it was common for the wealthy class to consider the work of serving tea to everyone as an honor and a duty.

A few years ago, I was able to have a formal afternoon tea at a beautiful establishment. The hostess taught us exactly what to do to serve and enjoy a restful time of tea and scones. Her very first question to our party was, "Who will serve the tea?" That person was taught how to strain the tea, how to pour, how to serve, and what to say. It was an honor. In the same sense, I believe it is a trustworthy position to be chosen as the person who manages the household accounts. It requires work. But it can be done in such a way that it brings peace and blessing to the family.

Is it possible for us to take the time and effort required to do the job well? Is it possible to be called trustworthy, dependable, and honorable as the one who is chosen to handle money? I think we can do it well if we focus. We should set up a routine to study and learn while carefully seeing to the needs of the household.

Have you been chosen as the one to handle an old fashioned budget? I hope this book will help.

**An Old Fashioned Budget**

# A Simple Budget

## 3

Years ago, it was not common to have every detail of spending listed in the budget. There were basic expenses including such things as rent, heat, and insurance. When a household was first set up, a home was chosen in an area the husband could afford. Do you remember hearing a young man say, "I need to be able to support a family before I get married." He was conscientious and planned in advance. As soon as he had a good position in business, or secured a farm to run, he felt he was ready to get married.

Over time, the family expected to prosper, gain financial security, and attain more material goods. They often started out with very little, a plan, and a great deal of hard work. It was necessary for the money to be properly managed to help prevent ruin and hardship in the case of foolish decisions. This included making wise decisions of what to buy or how often to save.

Their choice in that first little home made a great deal of difference in getting through the good and bad seasons. The expenses needed to be low and what the household could manage based on the income. It was not a good idea to take on obligations (such as debt or an expensive farm) based on a current amount of a good income. It was better to spend less, buy a lower cost home, and then be able to weather the storms when times got rough. (Times always got rough!) This is why it is important to set up a simple budget - a basic level of spending that will help see a family through the many changes in life.

Modern financial experts advise us to include certain items in a budget which were not common in old fashioned homes. I will list some of them here with an explanation of why they would not enter the minds of thrifty families in past generations. These are spending categories for "Entertainment."

These days it is so common to need money for our recreation. We watch paid television programs, purchase movies, pay for concerts, go out to eat at restaurants on a regular basis, and spend money on vacations.

These are not practical items for old fashioned, humble living. In my childhood home, we would not have dreamed of paying for television. As for movies, I don't think my parents ever attended a movie in their entire lives. It was an expense that didn't interest them. It was not common. Today it seems so normal to rent movies, attend the theater, and pay for our programs at home. While there is nothing wrong with enjoying one's free time, these expenses are not

**An Old Fashioned Budget**

basic needs. A category of this sort would not have been given for this type of spending.

When it comes to eating out at restaurants, this would have been a very rare event. Perhaps it only happened for a special occasion, such as a 25th anniversary dinner. It would have been something out of the ordinary that didn't happen very often. Many of us grew up eating home cooking that was comforting and nourishing. We preferred eating at home. On very rare occasions, after many years of good financial management, it may have been a treat to go out for lunch or dinner. It was also possible to be treated to breakfast "out" when staying with a relative. But restaurant meals were not part of a normal expense in a simple budget. It is always going to be more economical to eat at home.

Saving up for vacations, or going away on trips, is considered a normal part of life these days. But, in fact, these were considered luxuries in times past. Families who were of the upper class chose to have "holidays" and "trips" for rest and entertainment. It was not part of a simple budget for the frugal home. Most journeys, or times of traveling, happened when one was visiting relatives. There was little expense, other than gas for the car. Families would pack their pillows, blankets, and a basket of food to drive for hours (or even a couple of days) to get to Grandmother's house, or to visit an Uncle's home. You were hosted there and fed and taken care of as their guest. This type of trip was never called a "vacation." It was simply "visiting relatives."

**An Old Fashioned Budget**

If one wanted to attend a concert or symphony event, it was a rare privilege. One would have to go out of their way to come up with extra money outside of the budget. This was because it was not considered a basic need. Life was enjoyed in much more simple ways that did not cost money. There would be walks in the neighborhood to visit a nearby lake (or the sea, depending on where one lived). The sights of nature and the landscape brought one peace and joy. We do need times of recreation. We do need culture and experiences that bring good things to our lives, but they do not require spending money for the humble family.

For those of limited means, it would have been an occasional expense to purchase books or subscribe to a magazine. These were much desired luxuries that required patience and diligence to come up with extra money (outside of a basic budget) for such a rare treat. One would have to make a serious effort to obtain the funds for good literature. Thrifty experts suggest using the library for free entertainment. But in rural areas it is more difficult to get to a library to borrow and return books. Even then the selection and resources are more limited compared to large suburban libraries.

What does that leave for us to list in a simple budget? These were very basic and necessary expenses. These would be such items as: Rent (or mortgage), Electricity, Heat, Telephone, Insurance, Garbage Removal, Groceries, Gas for car, Charity (tithe), and Savings. Please notice there is nothing listed for retirement, college, debt,

**An Old Fashioned Budget**

repairs, personal spending, gifts, or clothing. There is a very important reason. I will go into more detail on this in the chapter, "We'll Get By."

## We'll Get By

### 4

My childhood home, in Massachusetts, was owned by my grandparents. They had raised their children, including my mother, in that same house. I was three years old when Mother, Dad, and we children moved in with our grandparents. We were given the main part of the house, while our grandparents settled into an attached apartment on the first floor. They were getting older and needed my Mother's help. This was a humble, old fashioned home on an acre of land. It was a beautiful neighborhood, in a suburb of Boston. Some years later, my grandparents went to be with the Lord, and Mom inherited the house.

The house was simply decorated in an old fashioned way. The furniture was old but well kept. The wallpaper was charming. We never imagined anybody redecorating or buying new things, unless it was necessary. I remember receiving a bedroom set as a gift from a relative. A new crib and nursery set was given to our household when my younger sister was born. Other than maintenance and repairs, my father did himself, we kept the house just as it was when our grandparents had raised their own children. It never entered our

**An Old Fashioned Budget**

minds to "upgrade" or to "make changes." We did the work of keeping things clean and neat. We were content and comfortable. This was the old style of living, which seems almost unheard of in these days.

When we spend money in ways that are not practical, in ways that are not essential, we lose money that is needed for basic needs that come up later in life – such as car repairs, clothing, or a tax bill. This is why it was not common to redecorate, or buy things on a whim. Money was not to be spent in a frivolous, impulsive manner. We did not buy a new refrigerator or a new stove unless it had been repaired many times and was no longer working. These days, we are taught to buy new appliances, new lamps, new furniture, and new home accessories to make us happy! This was unheard of in past generations.

Modern budgets include monthly cash for a variety of spending that makes managing money more difficult and, at times, unrealistic. I would like to share some of these here and explain some alternative ideas.

I have heard of middle class and wealthy families having a college fund for their children. Clearly this was something they could afford. But those living on a small income did not have the money to spare. I know many people who have never gone to college. Others have worked their way through school and had their children do the same. They also counted on scholarships or chose training programs

**An Old Fashioned Budget**

to help obtain a higher education. A humble, old fashioned budget does not list college money as a basic need. While education is essential to all of us, it does not always have to cost money. We have also noticed, from examples in history, how many have earned their own money to pay for school. They developed a sense of responsibility in the process. I have heard of older brothers working to put younger siblings through college. The need was met when they were presented with the struggle. This type of work ethic, and compassion for others, is incredible.

The greatest way of saving money for old age, was simply paying off the mortgage on the family home. Eliminating all debt was the best way to reduce expenses. For those who have a higher income, saving for retirement makes sense. But the old fashioned, simple budget did not have the funds for the future. There is nothing wrong with doing our very best, working hard, and being careful with one's money and simply trusting the Lord to provide our daily needs. This was a common way of life in past generations. We trust the Lord for tomorrow and just do our very best at being careful with the funds with which He provides today.

In my mother's day, there was no need to have a walk-in-closet. Personal possessions were limited. That was a common way of life for most people. They were happy and content and knew no other way. There was a small selection of "good" clothes for church and special events. There were also seasonal items to keep warm in winter and to stay cool in the summer months. Budgets, in those

**An Old Fashioned Budget**

days, did not have a monthly clothing allowance. New clothes were not being constantly added to the wardrobe. These days I am so surprised to see the constant shopping for used clothes at thrift stores and yard sales. We should certainly buy things when we need them, at the best possible price (used or new) but we should be mending and making things last, keeping our clothes pretty and clean, for as long as possible. Clothing and shoes, in old time budgets, were only purchased when necessary. It was not a basic need to have new things every month of the year.

I remember watching an old episode of *"The Waltons."* One of the children needed a new pair of shoes. They had saved up for this until there was enough money to buy them. This mind-set was so common in my childhood home, and especially in my own home as my children were growing up. It was a time before easy credit and consumer debt made it too easy to get everything that was needed immediately, before the money was even earned and saved. This is why you will not see a "clothing" category in old time budgets. The money for this need had to come out of the savings.

A humble family does not usually have access to an allowance for spending and gifts. These items are not on a simple budget. If one had money to spend (other than for basic needs or bills) it was thought that one must be wealthy. That was the common mind-set from past generations. If you needed to buy a gift, you would save up for it, over time. Even then, the gift was often practical or something inexpensive (or homemade) that was much appreciated.

**An Old Fashioned Budget**

I realize, in these modern days, people tend to need money to spend each day for the coffee shop, work lunches, etc. May I offer a suggestion? How about investing in a good quality thermos? Make coffee at home and then fill the thermos to take along with a packed lunch. Wouldn't that be charming? My father had a "Stanley Classic Lunch Box." It had a dome lid with a metal bracket to securely hold a thermos of nice hot coffee. Inside the main portion of the box was plenty of room for a couple of sandwiches, a banana, and a donut or coffee cake. It was as if he carried a nice picnic from home every time he went to work!

We children were taught to never leave home without some emergency money. It was not to be spent, like an allowance. It was only for a crisis. We had a dime for a pay telephone call, and a couple of quarters in case we needed to take the bus. Adults would have dollar bills kept in a purse or wallet. It was never spent, unless there was an emergency.

Each family will use their own judgment in deciding what is essential for their daily living. But in old fashioned budgets, a personal allowance was not usually listed as a basic need. People just did not spend all the time the way they do now.

I need to mention debt (any loan other than a home mortgage). Owing money used to be considered a burden. It was necessary to be relieved of that burden in the quickest possible way. To come up

**An Old Fashioned Budget**

with money to pay off that burden, spending was temporarily limited to very basic needs. There may not have been much extra money available for luxuries, gifts, visiting relatives, buying treats, or getting new clothes. All bills were cut as low as possible to manage on a small income. Sometimes things were sold to pay off a debt. Or, more often than not, extra work was done to earn more money. It was not considered a normal way of life to owe money for a long period of time. It was also considered questionable (or frivolous) if one spent money that could have been used to pay back a loan. If you have a fixed payment of debt, you will have to add that to your budget. But please consider adding some of your savings to that payment to eliminate the burden as quickly as possible.

These days many home mortgages include homeowner's insurance and property taxes. For those who do not have any debt on their house, they have to save up to pay these necessary bills. In an old fashioned budget, money is saved each month (ideally) for many things. But it is all lumped into one listing – savings. Money is then carefully taken out, as needed, for car repairs, home maintenance, taxes, etc. If Mom needs new winter boots, because the ones she has had for five years have finally given out, the money is taken out of savings to pay for it. Often the new boots are beautiful and sturdy and are like a gift that brings her a great deal of joy. Have you ever heard of a Mother making do with an old, worn coat each winter? Then on her birthday she is given a lovely new one that she will cherish for many years. In our culture today, we get new things so often, it is hard to bless someone with a birthday or Christmas gift.

**An Old Fashioned Budget**

Nobody seems to wait for things anymore. Nice things are treasured so much more when we wait until there is money available.

Repairs, clothing, shoes, taxes, gifts, etc. are funded when absolutely essential, from either savings, the sale of some item, a small portion taken from the grocery money, or extra cash earned from overtime pay. This is why the basic, simple budget does not list every single possible item one might need in life. We simply save all we can, all year round.

It takes practice to be content, to make do, and to do without until there is money available. This is when a gentle smile and the trusting words of, "We'll get by," bring a sense of peace to our lives. I have heard this said many times by husbands and wives. "We'll get through this," they say with great faith and trust in the Lord. "It will be okay." There is a humble joy in knowing that God will take care of them. We are promised enough just for today. Tomorrow will bring another blessing.

## Yankee Thrift

5

I think spending, in our modern culture, has become a habit in daily living. Many "live to spend" rather than just simply "live." It causes a life of stress and a constant focus on money, both in earning as much as possible and spending as much as possible. We will always want things. The world is full of a great variety of beautiful and useful things we can purchase. Yet our life cannot have its sole purpose in shopping and accumulating material goods. It reminds me of a small child in a department store. Perhaps it is a sweet little girl who is delighted at all the wonderful things displayed, aisle-after- aisle. You will hear her "oooh" and "ahhh" and point out many good things. Maybe the family is there looking for a gift for her little brother. But the little girl sees so many wonderful things she cannot help but want, that she starts to cry! It can be overwhelming and sad!

In my childhood days, it was not common to see products for sale all the time. We children simply did not go to the store. Our mothers did all the grocery shopping when we were in school. It was also more difficult to travel to a department store. They were not close to residential areas, in our Massachusetts town. This was because people did not commonly shop as frequently as they do now. There was not a "need" to have a great many stores for people to recreationally browse and spend. The family was more "home" focused and traditionally minded - in that they spent time on activities rather than on spending their money. It was also more common to live simply on a limited income. Why would one want to earn more money, in order to spend, when they could just enjoy their home and family time? They did not have the thinking we do in this modern day, when it comes to earning and spending.

These days, we have so many nearby stores and even online shops offered to us that we can, literally, browse and spend any time of the day or night! This is certainly overwhelming. Yet, when I was a child, shopping was greatly limited to us all. I never heard of a thrift store until after I was married. Yard sales were not anywhere near as common as they are these days. This was something I learned about when I was a young wife and mother. It may even shock you to hear that there was no such thing as Black Friday sales in previous generations. The first time I head of this advertising term was around fifteen years ago. I am used to the days of my childhood when Thanksgiving, and the few days after, were spent at home enjoying rest and family time. No one in our neighborhood thought about spending money during those days.

The main way we were exposed to shopping was from the old time Sears catalog. I believe a thick, large copy was in just about every single house. We kept ours in the cabinet of an end table in our

**An Old Fashioned Budget**

living room. If we wanted to "browse" or "dream about" buying something, we would sit on the floor and just look at all the toys, home décor, clothing, furniture, and anything else we wanted to see. But we never bought any of it! It was not convenient to fill out an order form, get a check ready, and place it in the mail. Then the wait for a few weeks before a package arrived gave us a sense that buying anything took a great deal of time. Our parents, of course, would order things a few times a year – for Christmas or a birthday. But again, this took time. It was not easy to just spend money like it is today. This gave us a great sense of patience, contentment, and appreciation for those rare times when we were given a gift, or able to purchase something. This is prudent and simple living that was common a couple of generations ago. It is old time Yankee thrift. We, who lived during that time period, knew no other way. It was a normal way of life.

I want to share a couple of examples of prudence taken straight from one of the First Ladies at The White House during the 1940's.

Bess Truman became First Lady, of the United States, in 1945. She was frugal and prudent, as most wives were in those days. According to the Chief Usher, she made sure her daughter had skills in homemaking, including the necessity of sewing. She wanted her daughter to know how to take care of her possessions, to avoid waste, and to have the skills to do many things herself – without cost. Of course, staff at The White House was accustomed to doing all of these things for the residents. Mrs. Truman could have easily

**An Old Fashioned Budget**

given much of this work to the employees, but she felt it was her responsibility and wanted her daughter to be capable as well.

These days, it seems, the basic job of sewing on a button, or mending a torn seam in clothing, is left undone because of a lack of knowledge. I was intrigued to read that even the linens, at The White House, during the Truman's residency, were mended and repaired by the staff.

Are you familiar with mending towels, pillow cases, curtains, and clothing? This is part of being thrifty. It is an important way of doing things for ourselves that do not cost money. Some of us have towels which are well worn and carefully mended. The purchase of new things for the house does not happen on a regular basis. We keep mending, washing, and repairing our possessions until they are no longer usable. It is then that we take a careful amount from savings and buy something new (when funds are available). We do not buy the best or the cheapest. We choose good quality items that will last a long time.

It has also been said that Mrs. Truman was just as careful about White House expenses as she was about her personal bookkeeping. There was a prevalent attitude, during that time period, that one must be careful to avoid waste or foolish spending. I have also seen this wise oversight in the writings of Jane Austen novels. It was not spending itself that was a problem, but a careless spending that wasted money. Money is not intended to be thrown around. It is to

**An Old Fashioned Budget**

be used with foresight and frugality. One can have a sense of practical elegance if one finds a way to enjoy life while being very careful with one's finances.

In Old Yankee Culture, here in New England, people do not want to part with their money. They live as simply as possible, with little expense as possible, so that money is available for those inevitable "rainy days." Yankee living has been studied extensively by those seeking to live on less. They are tired of seeing the pressure, the stress, and the burden of those struggling in a culture of debt.

Some of the characteristics of a person with strong Yankee values include the following:

They stay away from stores unless they genuinely need something. A trip to the store is very rare and they must have a specific product in mind to purchase. Old time Yankees do not window shop or spend time at the mall for recreation. They do not browse around looking to see what is available. They will not buy anything on a whim or just because it looked like it was a bargain. If they did not consider it a basic need, they would not spend their money. This does sound a bit extreme these days, but when money is limited it is good to learn how to manage until finances improve. (Honestly, I wish I had a stronger dose of this style of Yankee restraint!)

They are not known to eat gourmet food or spend time at restaurants. They do not seek out a variety in their choice of menus.

**An Old Fashioned Budget**

They tend to enjoy plain, nourishing, home-cooked food. They are very practical and live simply. They find happiness in home, family, and faith, rather than in what money can buy for them.

If something is broken, they will spend as much time as possible doing their own repairs. It is not uncommon to get a glimpse of duct tape on a window screen (discreetly done, of course). If absolutely necessary, they will pay for repairs. If money is not available, they will find a way to go without.

They have an ability to endure hard times with a great deal of patience. This is an incredible quality for many reasons. With regard to money, it prevents them from rushing out and solving every problem with money. They tend to find creative solutions, or wait out the trial until things improve.

They prepare in advance, as much as possible, for the coming season. For example: They know it gets very cold each winter. So they make sure they have firewood, or money for heating oil, at least a few months before the freezing weather begins. They also make sure they have warm clothing, coats, and gloves. They take care of these items so they will last many years. They are not often surprised by an unexpected expense. They tend to have what they need, including a little money to meet these trials of life.

Clearly it takes a great deal of self-discipline to live this way. It is admirable and something many of us will always need to work on.

**An Old Fashioned Budget**

While it is certainly a blessing to have occasional treats and luxuries, it is also important to be practical and careful in both good and bad times.

Yankee quote for tough times:

"There was no visible distinction from the 'haves' and the 'have nots' in our school, because everyone was a 'have not.' . . . No one had electricity. . . Most houses in the back country were in great need of paint. . . Hard work accomplished much of what there was no money to buy. . . Every housewife spent her evenings and every other spare moment mending, darning socks, turning worn collars and cuffs, repairing holes in sweaters, and sewing patches on garments that were coming apart. . . 'Eat it up, wear it out, make it do, or go without" was the code of the hills."  - *"Fetched up Yankee"* by Lewis Hill (A Vermont Author).

## Bookkeeping for the Home

### 6

Every business has someone in charge of accounting. They keep track of all the income and all the money that is spent. A company can quickly fail if the money is not carefully managed. It used to be that the finances in a home were just as carefully monitored. In the last several decades, there have been so many changes in the availability of easy credit, loans, and new banking technology that it can be overwhelming. Our culture tends to encourage us to have a great deal of free time for recreation. In order to "have a good time," we are getting the message that we ought to do important things, like bookkeeping, as fast as possible to get them over-with. It seems like training in careful skills of analyzing and planning are not very popular. But someone must keep the books, whether it is in a business or in a home. We must make time for this important work.

I sincerely believe that only one person should be in charge of the books. If both the husband and the wife are taking out money, paying bills, and managing things their own way, it will cause conflict and confusion. This is because everyone has their own method and way of doing things. I believe they can work together to

**An Old Fashioned Budget**

set up their plans, but then just have one person oversee the management aspect of the money itself – this includes handling the banking, paying the bills, and monitoring the budget and savings plan. I want to share some fictitious narratives to show you what this could be like. In the first case, the husband will be the one in charge of the bookkeeping. In the second example, the wife will be handling the money. (In each of our homes we need to make our own decision of whether Mom or Dad will be in charge of the finances. It really doesn't matter, as long as the chosen one is diligent, careful, and takes the job seriously.)

Before I share the sample stories, I have to make something very clear. When I refer to someone as being in Charge of the money, they are not the Boss, nor are they in Control. They are simply the designated overseer of all the many jobs required to keep the finances in order. This includes opening the bills that come in the mail, sorting them, setting up a plan to make payments on time, depositing and cashing checks, balancing the checkbook, recording entries in the checkbook registry, keeping the balance updated by doing the math as each transaction happens, etc. The chosen bookkeeper is simply the one who does the office work for the home.

Example One – "The husband as the chosen bookkeeper."

(George and Mary Chandler are the parents of 4 year - old twin girls, Mabel and Lucy. The season is winter.)

**An Old Fashioned Budget**

"Is there money available for new boots for Mabel?" Mary looked over at her husband. They were sitting at the breakfast table finishing up their coffee. "I have already patched them up a few times. The hole just keeps getting larger. Her poor little toes get soaked in the snow whenever we go out."

"Let me just get the bank book real quick." George got up from the table and soon returned with a calculator, note-pad, and a bank book. "How much do you need?"

"I believe $20 will be enough." She put the two girls on the sofa and gave them each a book to read.

"Yes, we have enough in savings for that. I do have another concern I wanted to talk about. We are running low on wood for the fireplace. I think one more cord will get us through until spring. But it will cost $250." George looked at the bank book and made a few notes on the paper.

Mary settled herself at the table with another cup of coffee. "I thought we had $500 put aside for the year. Could we take the money out from the savings?"

"That's exactly what I was thinking. I have been offered a few hours overtime for the next couple of weeks. I can put the extra income back into our account to build that money back up. Okay, yes. That's what we'll do."

The next morning, George ordered a cord of wood to be delivered. Mary took the twins to a local department store to buy Mabel a good, sturdy pair of boots.

All was well.

-----

Example two – "The wife as the chosen bookkeeper."

(Ben and Elizabeth Smith are the parents of one 10 year - old boy, Harry. The season is summer.)

Ben had just finished mowing the front yard. He walked into the kitchen for a cold drink. He smiled at Elizabeth and said, "I could really use a new lawn mower. We've had this one for 10 years and it was second-hand to begin with. I don't think it will last much longer."

"Do you think we could afford it?" Elizabeth suspected there was not enough money in savings to cover such a large expense.

"I don't know," said Ben. "Where do we stand financially?"

"I'll look over the books after lunch. Are you ready to eat?" She led her husband to the table and they enjoyed a pleasant time with Harry.

A short time later, Harry and Ben went outside to play basketball. Elizabeth took advantage of the quiet and pulled out her house accounts. She had a notebook for the budget, a calculator, her money jar of coins, and two bank books – for checking and savings. After doing a little math, she had a good grasp of their financial situation.

Elizabeth sat out on the back porch. She motioned for her husband to join her. "I looked over the books," she told him. "How much would the new mower cost?"

"Well," answered Ben. "There is a sale over at Kendall's. A good model would cost about $200."

"Well, here is what we have," started Elizabeth. "There is $20 in quarters in my money jar. I have $100 left of the grocery money for the month. There is enough money in the bank to cover all of this month's bills. And there is $300 in the savings account."

"It sounds like there is enough to buy the lawn mower." Ben looked over at Harry, who was still playing with the basketball. "But we would not have much left for an emergency or more groceries. I believe it is best for me to keep fixing up the old mower

**An Old Fashioned Budget**

and we can plan to save up for a new one next summer. How does that sound to you?"

Elizabeth looked relieved. "I think that's a very good idea. I appreciate your doing the extra work and waiting until there is more money available."

Ben nodded. "I appreciate your keeping such good track of our finances."

All was well.

-----

I realize both of these stories sound too ideal. But the concept is important. Whoever is doing the bookkeeping can help the family make good financial decisions.

## Money Diary

### 7

If we keep track of our spending we will have the accountability, or method of proving, for what happened to the money. A diary is a place where we write down the daily, or weekly, events of our lives. This is how we remember things. In the old days, a diary was called "a remembrance book." In the same way, if we write down the money we spend in a notebook or "Journal," we can analyze and solve many problems that may come up in our bookkeeping.

I will list several common questions that will help explain how this can work:

**First** – How can a history of our spending be beneficial?

One way this can be useful is by planning for future spending. Have you ever wondered how much you spent on oil to heat your home last winter? You can look back and see that, perhaps, in December you paid your supplier $250 and in February you paid

$400. (These are realistic numbers in colder climates.) This information will help you save extra throughout the year to cover the bills next winter.

Another benefit is that we can look back over the numbers and remember many events and happy times just based on how we spent our money. You might see an entry of "$20 to the department store for Betsy's birthday gift." Or perhaps a description of: "$10 to our church for the Deacon's Fund." You will also get a great deal of satisfaction seeing the bills being paid with entries like: "$650 to the bank to pay the mortgage" or "$75 to the electric company." With every entry, you are creating a history of your daily financial living. This is a blessing to see, and a comfort to know, everything is on track.

**<u>Second</u>** – Why is it important to write down every dime you spend?

It is important to have a budget, to keep your bank accounts in order, to organize your bills, and to stay on top of your home's financial matters. It is also important to keep track of every dime you spend. Every business does this. They must keep track and be aware of where the money goes. Otherwise, they are poor handlers of money. Shouldn't a home and family also take just as much care with their funds by keeping a money diary?

By taking the time to write down everything you buy, it will cause you to stop and evaluate whether or not the expense is reasonable. It makes you really think about what is happening to the money.

The diary of spending should also be made available to both the husband and wife. They both should be able to see where the money is going. However, keep in mind that some husbands don't really care about looking over the finances. That's okay! It is not necessary to share all the details, unless that is what your family wants to do. But please consider this - For those who want to hide their spending - Are they being wasteful? Are they mismanaging the money? If you are willing to share with your spouse, you are more likely to be careful, following the plans and goals for your household. Handling money is a responsibility and should not be taken lightly. It takes work but it is also a great honor.

**Third** – What kind of diary should I use?

Some use a plain notebook (or a fancy one), with the date, description, and amount spent listed on each line. From what I understand, Sarah (the wife of puritan minister, Jonathan Edwards) kept track of all her household spending on the backs of scrap paper. These were saved by the family, and later found by historians. This was in the 1700's. Sarah was considered an excellent manager of her home's economy.

Some like to use computer software and other modern technology. Personally, I like to keep an old fashioned, hardcover "journal." This is something that comes from an office supply store. It has "2 columns" and is published by "Boorum & Pease™." One book will last me four or five years. It is sturdier than a plain notebook. It also stands out to me that it is something specific. I also love the columns and find it easy to handwrite the entries. I prefer to use this old- time book because it takes little effort. I can just pick up the "journal" and flip through the pages to read, or just sit at a desk (or table) to do the writing. There is no need for electricity or a computer for this. It is the most simplified method available.

**Fourth** – How does this work?

If one person is handling the bookkeeping, one person should be writing in the money diary. Here is where all the spending is recorded - as it happens. It is proof that the budget is working. It is the answer to "where did all the money go?" It shows what happened to every dime. We write down the bills we pay. We record the debit transactions (such as $30 was spent on gas using the debit card.). We write down the checks we've written. We can find that information from our checkbook register. We just copy that same information into our money diary. We save our receipts for cash transactions and write them in the book. (Be sure to ask for a receipt. Not every company automatically hands them out anymore.) You might have several receipts from a week's worth of expenses. Just have a scheduled time to do your money diary work.

Take out these receipts and copy them into the Journal. Simply copy the date (from the slip of paper), the name of the store, a quick description, and the total. (There is no need to write down everything you purchased. Just write the total.) For example: "January 2, 2019, Rose's Country store – Groceries - $50."

For those times when it is not possible to get a receipt, try to keep a little notebook in your purse to jot down your spending as you go along.

**Fifth** – If the wife is doing the bookkeeping, does she write down the money her husband spends?

I never write down what my husband spends. I am only keeping track of what I (the bookkeeper) am doing with the money. If I give money to our grandchildren, I simply write something like "January 2, 2019 – Cash to Betsy - $3." It might be for something like school supplies. In the same way, if I give money to my husband, I will write, "January 2, 2019 – Cash to Mr. White - $30." I rarely write down a description of when he needs money because I am only responsible for what I do with the money. In this way, I am keeping track of where all the money is going, but I am not responsible for what others do with the money they spend. (They can certainly keep their own money diary if they would like.)

**An Old Fashioned Budget**

**Sixth** – Do you write down the income, or keep a running balance in the journal?

Unlike a checkbook register, you will not see an income listed in my journal. I do not balance income and expenses in my book. I only write down the money that is spent. This keeps the journal very easy to manage. Remember, there is only one purpose for the diary. That is to keep track of where the money went.

Below you will find an example of what you will see in my journal. I have placed a description in parentheses:

On the first page:

January 2019 (Month and Year)

| | | |
|---|---|---|
| 1/3 | Rose's Country Store - Groceries | $40 |
| 1/5 | Cash to Mr. White | $30 |
| 1/19 | Mortgage | $650 |
| 1/22 | Lost in Vending Machine | .25 cents |

(This will go on for an entire page or two as I write down the expenses as they happen throughout the month. At the end will be a total of all spending. I will start all over again on the next page for "February 2019," and on throughout the year.)

**An Old Fashioned Budget**

At the end of each month, I add up all the entries and put a total at the bottom of the page. It might say, "Total expenses this month - $1,340."

At times, it may seem tedious to write down all the spending. Is it overwhelming, for example, to write down that I lost a quarter in the vending machine? This is something you can decide on your own. It should not be a burden to you. We may not always catch these little expenses. Just do the best you can. Over time, you may just come to think of this as a game or a fun hobby!

**Seventh** – Do you separate spending into categories?

I never separate anything into categories. I am not concerned with how much went to "transportation," "home maintenance," "utilities" or other titles of spending. I simply keep a money diary and look at the entire total at the end of each month.

There are many people who enjoy doing categories. They might like to have graphs, charts, and color-coded descriptions of percentages- of- money- spent in many areas. There is nothing wrong with doing this. Many companies have these types of financial presentations. They would take the information in the journal to create these types of documents. But as for me, I just want a simple journal. I want to see a total at the end of each month to let me know that I spent less than we earned. This will mean that I managed the money well, and that is enough for me.

**An Old Fashioned Budget**

In the appendix, on page 75, you will find a photograph of a handwritten journal. I have used the fictitious family of George and Mary Chandler, from the previous chapter, as the example. Remember that George was the designated bookkeeper. But for the money diary, let's pretend that Mary was in charge of the finances. In this way, we get to see how she spends her grocery money.

Mary has $400 each month for grocery shopping. She will buy all food, laundry detergent, soap, and anything else she needs out of this money. From her diary entries, you will see that she also used some of the money on the following: A treat for her children at a bakery, flowers to cheer up their sick grandmother, books for her girls at the dollar store, and a birthday gift for Mabel.

In the margin of the diary, you will see a note explaining that Mabel's birthday gift came from a thrift store. Mary happened to be doing her grocery shopping right near that shop and wanted to quickly see if there was anything suitable for a gift. She managed to find a beautiful child's tea set in a little wicker basket. It was still in its original box and looked brand new. At a cost of $10, Mary thought it would make a perfect birthday gift for her little girl. We will pretend that Mabel's birthday is not until March. By preparing well in advance, Mary will be able to get a few nice things, over time, at an affordable cost.

**An Old Fashioned Budget**

This type of spending, including buying treats at the bakery and getting flowers for a sick relative, is rare, but possible, by using some of the grocery money. Since Mary makes a great deal of her food from scratch, has a menu plan, and keeps a good supply of food on hand, she can afford to carefully spend a few dollars when necessary, as long as she stays within the budget.

You may also notice, from the diary, that George does not get any spending money. (There would have been an entry to say, "Cash to George.") That is his choice. He packs his lunches for work, stays close to home, and is happy with what he already has. He also keeps a small amount of cash in his wallet in case of an emergency. There may be things that come up throughout the year that he will want or need. This can be easily managed if both George and Mary plan in advance for such expenses.

**An Old Fashioned Budget**

## The Writing Desk

### 8

I have read, in old literature, of a writing desk. This was sometimes kept in the Father's personal library at home. Or, it may have been in the parent's bedroom. It had a locked drawer and the key was well hidden. This was where all the important office work happened. There were partitions for bills, account statements, bank books, pens, stamps, stationary, envelopes, and a calculator. This basic piece of furniture was the foundational place for bookkeeping in the home.

I was in an antique shop a few weeks ago. I saw two different desks. One had the front cabinet style, with hinges on both sides, that would pull down and create a writing table. The inside contained shelves and little drawers. The cabinet would be pushed back up and locked securely at the top of the desk.

The second desk was known as a roll-top. You would take the handle, in front, and roll up the piece into a holding area. Once this was open, partitioned shelves and drawers appeared. I can just imagine how easy it was to organize everything one needed to run a little office with so many different compartments. After the desk was closed and locked, the private financial matters of the household were kept safe from prying eyes and curious visitors.

I went into a furniture store and noticed there are brand new, modern versions of both of these antique desks. This tells me that, to this day, there are still people who are using this type of furniture.

For those of us who are not blessed with such a home treasure, we might have a regular desk. This is the kind that has a flat (table) top and several drawers in the front. Some of these have locked drawers as well. We can keep important files in these drawers to hold insurance policies, bank statements, and tax returns. Another drawer might hold the checkbook, the current bills, and our financial books – for the budget (composition notebook) and money diary (journal book). We all have our own method of managing our paperwork and bills, but wouldn't it be ideal to have an old-time writing desk?

A great benefit of having a special desk is that we are more likely to take our time doing the paperwork. We may enjoy sitting down at a designated, quiet spot, and analyze the budget. We might carefully write out each check (using our best cursive handwriting). We could check off each bill as it is paid, and balance all our accounts using the calculator. We would also have a place to discreetly store the "petty cash fund."

Here is where I want to talk to you about keeping our bank accounts balanced and striving to always know exactly how much

**An Old Fashioned Budget**

money we have. If all is in one organized place, it is so much easier to manage it all. I don't know of any other place better suited for bookkeeping than a desk.

In this chapter, I mentioned (for the first time) having a "petty cash fund." This is required in all businesses to handle a sudden, or fast, need of cash. A home needs the exact same thing. I will explain this in terms of avoiding overdrawing our bank accounts. In these modern days, banks offer us a "benefit" of having an overdraft protection service. It seems it is automatically assumed everybody wants this. But the truth of the matter is that it helps you get want you want (right now) even if you don't have the money in the bank. It is like a line of credit, for a fee, each time it is used.

A petty (meaning "trivial" or "tiny") cash fund will provide you with that money so you can avoid being charged a fee and going into debt with the overdraft program. This small sum of money can be kept, neatly and safely, in a locked drawer of your writing desk. (In the old days, in some homes, it may have been kept in a money jar, or cookie canister, in the kitchen.)

If you don't want the over-draft protection service, simply tell the bank to remove it from your accounts. This means that when you are using your debit card, and there is not enough money in the bank, the card will not work. In other words: You will not be able to buy anything because you don't have the money. This will save you from the burden of going into debt and paying fees. I realize it is a

**An Old Fashioned Budget**

convenience for many to use the service. But I want to share a couple of fictitious examples that may help us get through those times when we need a little extra money. This will be through the use of a petty cash fund, rather than relying on over-drafting the account.

Example One – George and Mary Chandler with the twin girls, from Chapter 6.

(This is the family that has George managing the household money.)

It is late in the evening. The girls have just been put to bed. Mary is at the kitchen table looking over the grocery store advertisements, making plans to shop the next day. She notices a special feature to help the needy. Customers can donate $5 or $10 and the store will use that money to purchase food to donate to the local food pantry. Mary knows how difficult it is to go without enough food and wants to help. Her budget for the week is $100. But she would like an additional $10 to help the hungry in her neighborhood.

George has just come home from a late staff meeting. "Are the girls asleep?" He asks his wife. He quietly heads over to the kitchen counter to get his dinner.

"Yes, I think so," answers Mary. "I kept your dinner warm. There is also a piece of apple pie for your dessert. It is the last piece. The girls had the rest of it this afternoon."

**An Old Fashioned Budget**

Mary, knowing their budget has been carefully planned for their family's security, hesitates to ask for more money. But she thinks they can manage to help the less fortunate whenever possible. She gets up to finish the laundry. "George," she lingers at the table. "I know you said there is $100 in the debit card account for my grocery shopping tomorrow. But I would like to have an additional $10."

"That's fine," he answers. "We won't have a chance to get to the bank, but I do have some cash available." He is talking about their petty cash fund. "We have about $30 right now. I can get the $10 for you after dinner."

"Will you be able to save some more money next payday to replace it?" Mary does not like the work of bookkeeping and wants to make sure it will not interfere with paying their current bills on time.

"It's no problem," says George. "Do you remember that we are saving about $25 each month for petty cash? It is designed to handle these types of situations."

Mary is relieved and happy that she can help others while still caring for her own family. She is also thankful that the expense is covered through George's careful management of their money.

All was well.

**An Old Fashioned Budget**

---

Example Two – Ben and Elizabeth Smith and their son, from Chapter 6.

(Elizabeth is the one who handles the money in this family.)

Ben was just called in to work on the morning of his day off. A co-worker is sick and will not be able to do his job. Ben tells his boss that he will be there as quickly as possible. At that moment, he remembers that he does not have any gas in his truck. He will need to use the debit card on his way to work.

"I need $40 for gas this morning," he tells his wife. This is his budgeted amount for the week and was expected.

Elizabeth quickly helps Ben get his work tools and uniform together. "Yes," she tells him. "There is enough in the bank to cover that."

Just before he rushes out the front door, he remembers he will need a packed lunch. There is no time for Ben or Elizabeth to prepare food for him. Ben tells her not to worry. "I will just spend $10 for lunch using the debit card."

Elizabeth knows they are on a tight budget and this would not be possible. "Ben, there isn't enough money in the account for that."

**An Old Fashioned Budget**

She thinks for a minute and then remembers the petty cash fund. "But I have $10 in cash I can give you."

Ben is happy with that, and is able to head to work without a worry.

All was well.
---

Again, these stories both sound simple- minded and ideal. But these types of situations are very common. If we can plan in advance, for these common daily problems, we can still manage the money well.

I want to draw your attention to the situation with George and Mary. Did you notice that Mary never mentioned why she wanted the extra $10? Also notice that George did not ask her to explain. This is a key aspect of trust and a willingness to allow each one to make their own decisions regarding the use of small amounts of money without explanation.

It was okay with this couple whether Mary gave $10 to feed the needy or if she wanted to spend the money on a bouquet of flowers for herself. They both trusted each other to do the right thing. They simply needed to know how much was spent, in order to properly manage their money.

**An Old Fashioned Budget**

In the case of a large expense, a couple should certainly make an agreeable plan they both would be happy with. It should be something that would not interfere with their budget.

Keep in mind that no amount of planning, or the use of a beautiful writing desk is going to eliminate money problems. We will have occasional emergencies and some times of crisis when there simply isn't enough money. But what we want to do is carefully take the time to handle the day-to-day happenings without constant stress and worry about going into debt. We want to avoid making little mistakes because we did not have a plan to avoid these problems.

Will a writing desk make a difference? Perhaps not, but if we have a designated, organized place to do the bookkeeping, we will be in a far better place than if we lived by whims in a forgetful, disorganized fashion.

# The Old Fashioned Budget

## 9

I want to share with you a basic budget. We will use the fictitious family of Mr. and Mrs. Chandler, from chapter 6, as our example. In this household, George is the one who does the bookkeeping for the family. But first I want to remind you that we are talking about low income families. These are not middle class or wealthy homes. These are people of humble means that, more than likely, will always be living on a small income. There are many people living in a similar way.

Most modern budgets talk about how to allocate your budget based on a percentage of your income. This is not realistic for humble families. Personally, I think the percentages confuse many of us and require a formula for managing money that doesn't make sense. A simple, old fashioned budget is easy to follow for those of any income. But it is especially useful for those of simple means. It lists all your necessary, basic expenses, along with a savings plan.

The old-time budget looks something like this:

Charity (a tenth, or tithe, of one's income.)

Mortgage or Rent – We will assume the home is low cost and affordable.

Electricity

Heat (Such as Oil, Propane, Kerosene, or Wood) or Air Conditioning - depending on where you live.

Telephone/ Internet (Internet has come to be a modern necessity in many homes.)

Insurance (Homeowners, Auto, and Life) - I want to mention that a humble family would have a basic life insurance policy that would provide enough money to pay for a burial (funeral). I have never heard of an old fashioned family (including those in the history of my own family) to have more life insurance coverage than a basic one for burial costs. I just do not want you to feel pressured to obtain large life insurance policies with premiums many cannot afford to maintain. It used to be common to live with low expenses, while avoiding debt. The need was a basic, small policy to pay for a funeral. This is something each family will have to decide what is best for their circumstances.

Garbage Removal

Gas for Car

Grocery – This has always included food and anything else one needs to buy at the store, such as trash bags, laundry detergent, etc.

**An Old Fashioned Budget**

Savings – (There are three categories for this).

**First Savings** are for yearly expenses, such as property taxes, car registrations, etc.

**Second Savings** are for a "rainy day" (or emergencies).

**Third Savings** are for the Petty Cash Fund.

Other – (this is where you can customize it to meet your needs. You might have debt payments or elementary school tuition for your children.)

Our budget is for the family of George and Mary Chandler. They have the twin daughters.

First, we need a little background on the family. George works in a small office and earns $1,800 per month. This is their only income. He is paid bi-weekly at a rate of $900 each paycheck. (This is his take-home pay after deductions.) His family has a mortgage on their home, but no other debt. The twins are homeschooled. Mary and the girls are content to stay home most of the time, which saves them money. She only uses $15 per week to put gas in her car. George lives a short distance from his job. He needs $30 each week for gas.

They live in a cold climate and are on a "budget plan" through their oil supplier. This means they pay a set amount each month, throughout the year, which is an average of their winter heating cost. The current amount is $70 per month. This is re-evaluated each year.

**An Old Fashioned Budget**

They own a small, humble house. The mortgage payment is $650 each month. This includes their homeowner's insurance and property taxes.

The couple pays their car insurance ($380) in full each year because it saves them money. They also receive a discount for paying it all up front. In order to do this, the money is put into a "yearly savings account." They also use this account to save for the annual renewal of their car registrations ($50 for each car). This yearly savings account is never used for any other purpose. In order to find out how much they needed, they simply added up the total of each yearly bill ($480) and divided that by 12 months. This gave them the $40 they need to save to cover these bills. They also know exactly which month each bill comes due so there is no surprise. This information can be found in a variety of ways: Searching last year's checkbook register, reading the money diary, looking in a folder containing the year's paid bills, or calling each company for details.

Their rainy day savings is $35 each month. This was calculated by taking whatever was left over after all other expenses were paid. If their income increases or there is some windfall – such as a tax refund, it would be added to this rainy day savings fund. This money is used for emergencies, repairs, essential clothing, or helping someone in need. (If one did not own a house, this money could be used towards a down payment.)

**An Old Fashioned Budget**

They have a main budget and a yearly expense worksheet.

Main Budget for George and Mary:

| | |
|---|---|
| Tithe - | $180 |
| Mortgage - | $650 |
| Electricity- | $ 75 |
| Oil Heat- | $ 70 |
| Phone/Internet- | $ 80 |
| Life Insurance- | $ 40 |
| Garbage Removal- | $ 25 |
| Gas for Cars- | $180 |
| Grocery- | $400 |
| Yearly Savings- | $ 40 |
| Rainy Day Savings- | $ 35 |
| Petty Cash Savings- | $ 25 |

Total  $1,800

This is the main budget they create as a guide to use throughout the year. However, a brand new budget is made each month because expenses will fluctuate. For example, the electric bill is not always the same. Also, there will be months when no yearly savings are listed but one of those bills will appear on the budget. For example, if their car insurance (an annual bill) is due in June, their budget will have this expense listed but direct them to take part of the payment from savings. Once each bill is paid, or each expense happens, George (as the bookkeeper) will cross them off throughout the month.

**An Old Fashioned Budget**

In the middle of the year, the income might increase. In this case they will want to add that extra amount to the "rainy day savings account." The budget directs and guides them to manage the money well. This is why they write a fresh new one each month so they can keep track and follow the plan, making notes, and crossing off items as they are taken care of.

Here is their Yearly Expense worksheet:

Car Insurance $380 - (Due in June)
Car Registration renewals $100 ($50 each) – (Due in February)

Next, it is important to break down the monthly bills to make it easy to pay them all. Since George is paid bi-weekly, we need to know HOW to divide up the money in order to pay the bills. We simply list the four weeks in the month along with the income for each week. Then we write down exactly what to pay.

There are two parts to each budget. The first one lists all of the expenses for the month (the "main budget" listed above.) It tells you WHAT to pay. The second part of the budget tells you WHEN and HOW to pay.

Here is the second part of the budget:
At the top of the page, write down the month and year. Then write the total income.

**An Old Fashioned Budget**

"January 2019"
"Income: $1,800 – paid bi-weekly"

Week One $900
Pay the following:

| | |
|---|---|
| Tithe - | $ 90 |
| Electric- | $ 75 |
| Phone/Internet- | $ 80 |
| Life Insurance- | $ 40 |
| Grocery- | $200 |
| Gas- | $ 90 (Put aside half of this for week 2.) |
| Save for Mortgage- | $325 |
| Total paid  $ 900 | |

Week Two  $ - 0 –
No bills to pay.

Week Three $ 900
Pay the following:

| | |
|---|---|
| Tithe - | $ 90 |
| Pay the Mortgage- | $325  (Add this to week one savings to pay the total.) |
| Grocery- | $200 |
| Gas- | $ 90 (Put aside half of this for week 4.) |
| Heat- | $ 70 |
| Garbage Removal- | $ 25 |
| Yearly Savings- | $ 40 |
| Rainy Day Savings- | $ 35 |
| Petty Cash Savings- | $ 25 |
| Total paid  $ 900 | |

Week Four $ - 0 –
No bills to pay.

**An Old Fashioned Budget**

To keep track of the budget itself, I like to use a plain composition notebook. I use two pages for each month. The left side is for part 1 of the month's budget. The second page, part 2, tells me when and how to pay the bills. Since I write a new budget each month, and use 2 pages per month, one notebook will last me about 6 years.

It is clear that George and Mary live on a small income. Their budget is very tight, with very little money available for savings. This is very common for many families living on limited means. Someday their mortgage will be paid off and this will free up a great deal of money. For this reason, we should be thinking of our homes as a form of savings for the future. A careful budget is an important plan to help them live within their means.

Just remember that no matter how rich or poor a family, if they do not maintain their bookkeeping, or follow a budget, their money will be mismanaged and wasted. This will cause them a great deal of marital conflict.

**An Old Fashioned Budget**

## A Trusted and Diligent Bookkeeper
### 10

In some of Jane Austen's novels, there is a poor family living on an annual annuity. This is their security which is supposed to last their lifetime. This may have happened suddenly, after some death in the family, or as a result of a financial crisis. They must make changes and adjust their living in order to survive for the long term. Some, who have been used to a few servants, must now do all their own housework. Others must move to a less expensive home in a cheaper town. They align their living according to their means. It is amazing to see those who are used to careful diligence in their expenses make an almost effortless change in circumstances to meet the need.

In *"Aunt Jane's Hero"* by Elizabeth Prentiss, a newly married couple lives in an unfashionable town with very little to get by. There are hardships and struggles, but the beautiful home-life (with serving the Lord as the focus) is a blessing to read.

**An Old Fashioned Budget**

It is almost romantic and charming to imagine a wife who has to live on little, cheerfully say to her husband, "Let's play at being poor for awhile!" She cheers her husband on to better days with her contentment in all circumstances. Most homes start out poor! I have also heard older couples, who are struggling with debt or overspending, say how much better it was when they first started out with very little. "Life was simpler then," they would reminisce.

I believe the key to managing money well, regardless of the circumstances, is to avoid debt by going without, learning to pray for our daily needs, saving up to pay for what we want, and living an ordinary, frugal life.

A few little thoughts of advice might help:

Considering Debt: Don't take on obligations in the good times. You may not be able to handle them in the bad times.

Keep your accounts in order, always knowing precisely how much you have to work with. Even in hard times, the bookkeeper ought to know where the household stands financially.

Make realistic goals. You don't want to struggle, or be crazy, trying to save 75% of a modest income. You have to have food. You have to be warm. You have to have a place to live.

**An Old Fashioned Budget**

As soon as you get paid: pay the bills, put money aside for savings, etc. Put all the money where it needs to go right away. When we wait, other things somehow come up, causing that cash to slowly disappear for little expenses. This would not have happened if the money had been sent, immediately, to where it was supposed to go.

Live as if you did not have any extra money. Stick to the budget.

Focus on the duty of keeping the books. Make the time and set up a schedule to pay the bills and maintain the money.

The well known minister, John Wesley, advised: "Earn all you can, save all you can, give all you can." I notice he did not say, "Spend all you can."

If you need something extra and do not have enough money, work extra hours, sell something, and take the time to save up until you have enough. Patience is an incredible virtue.

Never be pressured to buy something "right now." Even if you lose the opportunity for a good sales price, it is better to wait, losing the "deal" than to spend money on impulse or on a whim. Following a financial plan (the budget) helps keep us on a secure track.

Many people, in these modern days, don't experience hardship anymore. They overspend and get into debt to have everything "right

**An Old Fashioned Budget**

now." It used to be common to keep working, pray, and wait - to "stand still," with faith that the Lord will provide at the right time.

Re-evaluate your idea of what you really need. These days many are routinely spending $2 here and $3 there on little treasures and treats. They consider them good bargains. But if one could be happy without these purchases, a great deal of savings would build up over the years.

Avoiding debt will give you more freedom to easily change your circumstances in case you need to move to a less fashionable town, or lower your spending.

You can make a lovely home even in a cheap house if you make an effort at tidying, decorating with what you already have, presenting wholesome meals, and being a sweet and gracious hostess.

Remember to pray for our daily bread. We should pray for our needs each day. This is today's portion. It is a daily rate. The Lord will take care of us today. We must work hard but trust Him to do His part.

From what I understand, there are more wives managing the money than husbands. Research has also shown that women spend far more money than men. This is because we buy most of the food, clothing, etc. for the family. It would be such a blessing to be trusted and diligent in managing the family fortune. Even a small,

**An Old Fashioned Budget**

humble home is still considered an estate. Whether you live in riches or reduced circumstances, your household income should be managed well.

There are going to be times of poverty and times of riches in many homes. There are seasons for all things. If we live modestly, on a limited income, we are more capable of getting through the lean times. Please realize that there are many families who live on a humble income. They often live this way their entire lives. It is more common than we may realize.

A great many modern families today are burdened with consumer debt and are living an unrealistic, stressful life. Others are trying desperately to get rich quickly, or work an unrealistic amount of hours to provide far more than necessary. This strains the family and weakens the home. We do not have to live this way.

There is nothing wrong with living on a low income. If you happen to have more than a modest income, the goal might be just to save all the rest, or help the less fortunate. I believe our biggest problem these days is unbridled spending. Our priority must be the home, time with the family, and being productive with our days. We need to start "doing things" instead of "buying things."

The key to living on a limited budget is to be very precise and careful with one's money. This is why we need to have a capable bookkeeper for the home. I like to think of this person as the

**An Old Fashioned Budget**

secretary. She does the office work, in a quiet manner, behind the scenes. She is careful and respected in her work and she does it well.

Just like in a business, there is no ambition for the bookkeeper. Her job description is not coming up with ways to make more money. She is not taking risks or inventing get- rich- quick schemes. She is content and skillful with the wages. Her job is to properly manage the income her household is provided with. She does this to help her husband so that he has no need to worry. But most of all, she does the bookkeeping as a faithful steward of the money the Lord has put into her hands.

**An Old Fashioned Budget**

# Appendix

**An Old Fashioned Budget**

**An Old Fashioned Budget**

{Previous page} Photograph one.

Left – Composition notebook for the Budget.

Right – Journal (2 column ledger) book for the money diary.

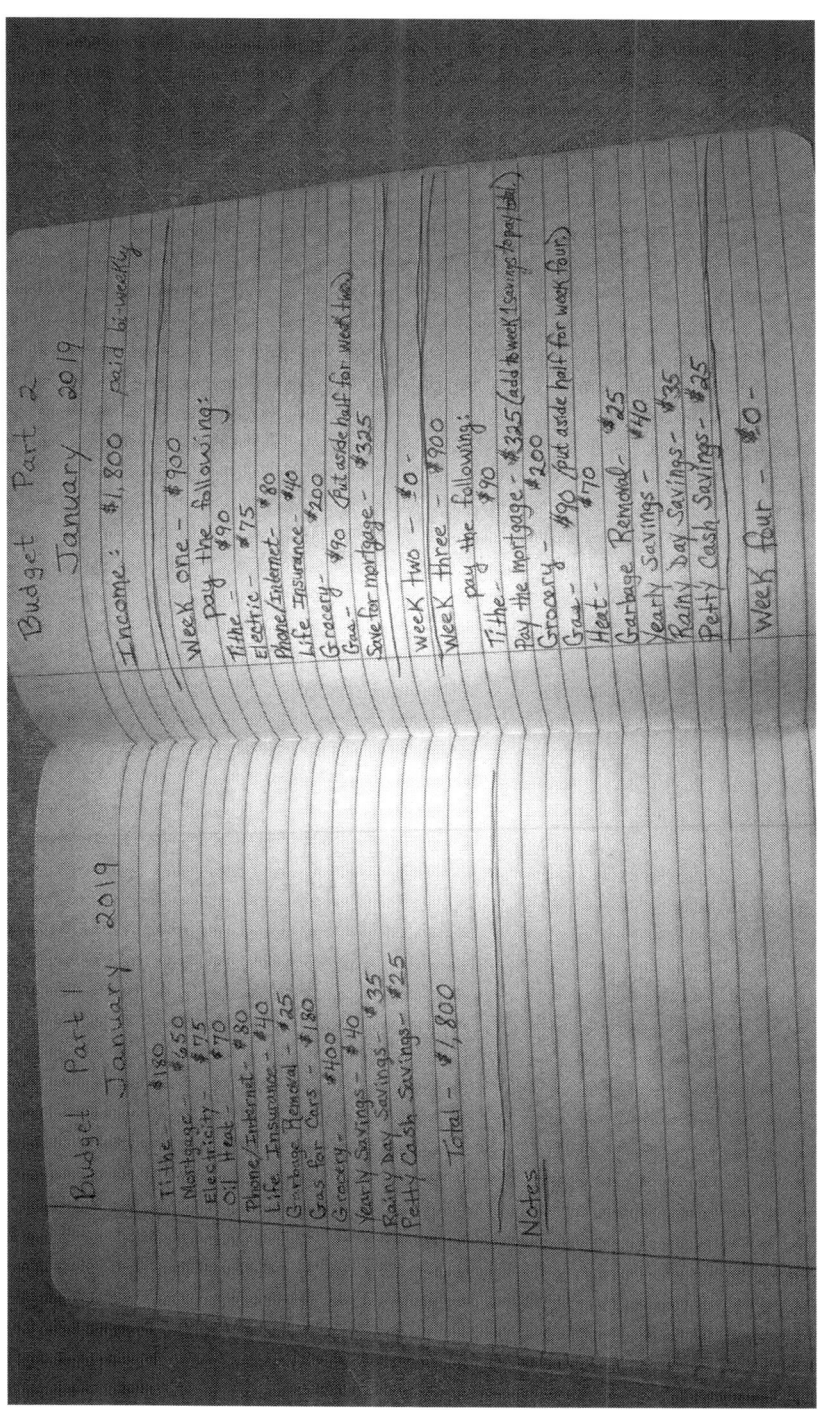

**An Old Fashioned Budget**

{Previous page} Photograph two.

Composition notebook showing the two - page budget for one month.

**An Old Fashioned Budget**

## January 2019

| | Date | Item | Amount |
|---|---|---|---|
| | 1/1 | Mortgage | 650.00 |
| | 1/2 | Cash to Mary | 10.00 |
| | 1/2 | Rose's country store (Grocery) | 160.10 |
| George | 1/4 | Gas for the car | 45.00 |
| | 1/4 | Electric bill | 75.00 |
| | 1/6 | Donation to Church | 90.00 |
| | 1/7 | Phone / Internet bill | 80.00 |
| | 1/7 | Mary's Life insurance | 20.00 |
| | 1/7 | George's Life insurance | 20.00 |
| Mary | 1/10 | Gas for the car | 24.00 |
| thrift store | 1/15 | Birthday Gift for Mabel | 10.00 |
| | 1/15 | Rose's Country Store (Grocery) | 79.35 |
| | 1/20 | Donation to church | 90.00 |
| | 1/21 | Heat bill | 70.00 |
| | 1/21 | Garbage Removal bill | 25.00 |
| | 1/23 | Florist Shop (to cheer up Grandma she's sick) | 12.00 |
| | 1/23 | The Baker's cafe (treat for the twins) | 10.00 |
| | 1/23 | Rose's country store (Grocery) | 101.07 |
| Mary | 1/28 | Gas for the car | 25.00 |
| | 1/28 | Department store (Boots for Mabel) | 20.00 |
| | 1/30 | Rose's country store (Grocery) | 23.40 |
| | 1/30 | Dollar store (books for Lucy + Mabel) | 3.18 |
| George | 1/31 | Gas for the car | 45.00 |
| | | **Total** | **1,688.10** |

**An Old Fashioned Budget**

{Previous page} Photograph three.

A sample page from a Journal (2 column ledger) book for the money diary.

## About the Author

Mrs. White has been a housewife for more than 30 years. She is the granddaughter of a revival preacher, Mother of 5, and a Grandmother of 10.

She has been writing about homemaking on her blog, "The Legacy of Home" since 2009.

She is a retired homeschool teacher from the Boston area. She lives with her family in an old 1850's house in rural Vermont.

For more information, or to find Mrs. White's books, please visit:

The Legacy of Home Press

**https://thelegacyofhomepress.blogspot.com**

Also see Mrs. White's blog:

**https://thelegacyofhome.blogspot.com**

Made in the USA
Middletown, DE
14 November 2019